M000080203

# The Psalms Were Made For Lent

## Six Sermons And Worship Services

### Robert G. McCreight

CSS Publishing Company, Inc.
Lima, Ohio

THE PSALMS WERE MADE FOR LENT

Scripture quotations are from the *Revised Standard Version of the Bible,* copyright-
ed 1946, 1952 (c), 1971, 1973, by the Division of Christian Education of the National
Council of the Churches of Christ in the USA. Used by permission.

Paraphrased Psalm hymns are reprinted from *Singing Psalms Of Joy And Praise,*
copyright 1986, by Fred R. Anderson. Used by permission.

**Library of Congress Cataloging-in-Publication Data**

McCreight, Robert G., 1948-
    The Psalms were made for Lent : six sermons and worship services / Robert G.
McCreight.
       p.   cm.
    ISBN 0-7880-0565-0 (pbk.)
    1. Lenten sermons. 2. Bible. O.T. Psalms — Sermons. 3. Sermons, American.
4. Worship programs. 5. Lent — Prayer-books and devotions — English. I. Title.
BV4277.M268    1996
264-dc20                           95-39883
                                           CIP

This book is available in the following formats, listed by ISBN:
0-7880-0565-0   Book
0-7880-0719-X   IBM 3½
0-7880-0720-3   Macintosh

*This book is dedicated to the people of the First Presbyterian Church in Marshall, Michigan, who so graciously invited me into their hearts and lives. Every pastor should have the privilege of serving in ministry with a congregation who so easily lives out the Christian faith.*

# Table Of Contents

# Preface

The Psalms have long been recognized as a rich resource for individual spiritual enrichment and for magnificent corporate liturgical expression in the life of the Church. But for many people the diversity of themes and styles in the Psalms has presented a stumbling block for their use and usefulness. This was certainly true for me personally, until I came upon Walter Brueggeman's helpful distinction of three separate types of Psalms which puts most of them into definable categories. My comprehension of this stirred me to teach the Psalms in a Bible study program and to preach a series of Lenten sermons which both educates about the types of Psalms and illustrates their truthfulness. This collection of six sermons is an attempt to translate some of the deep themes inherent in the Psalms into meaningful language and experiences which the person in the pew lives with.

Not content to leave it with that, I further developed this series on the Psalms by creating liturgical responses to match the categories of Orientation, Disorientation and New Orientation which Brueggeman proposes. I found the paraphrase of many Psalms which The Reverend Fred Anderson put to well-known hymn tunes to be a creative addition to further reinforcing the three themes in the worship experience. Thus each sermon comes with liturgical responses and three paraphrased hymns with singable tunes that make that worship service a unified experience. All together this resource invites the listeners in your congregation to experience the Psalms in a new and meaningful way.

7

# God's Plan
# For Your Happiness

## Psalm 1

**Introduction**

Several years ago I rented the video of a classic Broadway musical that I hadn't seen for quite a long time. I enjoyed watching the play by Jay Lerner, *Paint Your Wagon*. It's a musical comedy adventure story about the gold rush days in California of the last century. You may remember how it depicts the high experiences of finding gold buried in the ground and striking it rich. It depicts the loneliness of some of those hearty pioneer folk, and the sadness of dreams that never come true, despite years of hard work.

The scene that I best remember is a conversation in one of those low times, late at night on a muddy street of the frontier town. One man says to the other, "I guess there's two kinds of people in the world, Ben. People that move and people that stay. Ain't that true, Ben?"

And Ben says, "No, that ain't true." "Well, what is true?" asks the first man.

"There's two kinds of people," said Ben. "Them goin' somewhere an' them goin' nowhere. That's what's true." Then Ben went on to say, "I'm an ex-citizen of nowhere, an' sometimes I get mighty homesick."

**A**

I don't know that Ben had ever read the Psalms. But he stumbled onto a piece of wisdom that is shared by the psalmist whose words were read just a few minutes ago. That person or persons, whoever they might be, held the same point of view that there are two types of people in the world. And it's not that some are staying and some are going. Both types are going. Some are going somewhere, and the rest are going nowhere. And pity the people going nowhere. That's what the first psalm is about, and many later psalms espouse the same conviction. There are two types of people in the world, two ways to follow. Very simply, there is the right way — the way of God and the way of righteousness, the way of faith; and there is the wrong way — the way of falseness, the way of idolatry, the way of self-centeredness.

> *Some are going somewhere, and the rest are going nowhere. And pity the people going nowhere. That's what the first psalm is about.*

Today we take the first steps on a new path of our spiritual journey that will take us through the Lenten period and to Easter Sunday. There are 150 psalms, and obviously we can't deal with any more than a few. But through a selection of psalms which are the basis for a series of sermons we'll get acquainted with the diversity of psalms, and allow them in their richness to speak to us. Each week we'll sing the psalms and relive the vibrant conversations which the Hebrews of old had with God.

The texts for these sermons are each taken from the Book of Psalms, and grouped in one of the three categories suggested by professor and theologian Walter Brueggeman. Psalms of Orientation — the first category — portray a confidence in God's goodness to the faithful and hardship to the foolish and disobedient. The next category — the Psalms of Disorientation — challenge the notion that good things always come to good people. And finally, the Psalms of New Orientation come out of a situation of moving beyond the unfairness of life through a transformation and renewal of spirit.

Today we start with Psalm 1, the best place to start, because this psalm serves as a prologue to the entire Psalter. It is brief, simple, and to the point. The first three verses talk about people who are happy. And the reason they are happy is because they avoid evil people who have no use for God. Instead, they find joy in obeying the Law of the Lord. And because that is the nature of their living, their lives are characterized by fruitfulness and blessing and prosperity and well-being.

Then there are two verses about people who are not happy. And the reason they are not happy is that their choices for living reflect a turning away from God. Their lives are shallow; their character is thin.

The final verse in this psalm summarizes the point and concludes the passage. "The Lord watches over the way of righteousness, but the way of the wicked will perish."

**B**

There's an old Jewish bit of humor about the son who tells his father that he wants to marry Miss Katz. The father objects, saying that Miss Katz has no dowry. But the son insists that only with Miss Katz will he ever be happy. Thereupon the father says, "To be happy — and what good will that do you?" The point seems to be that in life (or at least in marriage) happiness is about as useful as the pursuit of wealth is desirable. But both the father and the son are after the same thing. They just disagree over how to obtain it.

In this psalm and others the presumption is identical. Humankind is not that unlike itself. We just differ over how we're going to get what we most want and need in life. Some think that the bluebird of happiness will be ours in the form of bigger barns to hold the accumulated possessions of living and striving. Others seek happiness in sexual exploits and chasing after other adventures of the senses. Still others look for

11

happiness through some form of control over others, whether it be military might or marital domination or something else. But everyone pursues some form of happiness.

But not all happiness is the same. And the wise person, presumes the psalmist, will be able to distinguish between short-term and long-term happiness, between happiness that titillates and happiness that nurtures the well-lived life, between real happiness and something else that gives the appearance of happiness.

> *It will help us, I think, to outline the impact of this little psalm around three points, or better, think in terms of three legs on a stool. The three legs of the stool that I have in mind are "knowing," "being," and "doing."*

It will help us, I think, to outline the impact of this little psalm around three points, or better, think in terms of three legs on a stool. The three legs of the stool that I have in mind are "knowing," "being," and "doing." If the psalmist were to stand before you this morning he would say that happiness is yours when these three elements are in place and balanced. Together, they prescribe God's plan for your happiness.

First there is KNOWING. What do we need to know in order to be happy? For the psalmists there was no question. The answer to that is clearly presented. The destination of happiness is not far away when we choose to follow the pathway of knowing the Law of the Lord, in Hebrew, the Torah.

The word *torah* means "law," but when we speak of law today we think in terms of absolutes, of external directives, or punishment when some statute is transgressed. That's not quite what the Hebrews mean by "torah." Torah to them is much softer and inviting. Torah is not tricky and rigorous. Rather, it is pragmatic, offering good insight into the practicalities of how best to live. Our best translation of torah might be "folklore." The Hebrews believed that there are certain appropriate, God-approved ways to keep yourself out of trouble and be relatively happy. It's called torah.

But simply knowing the torah isn't enough. The person must also believe in the torah. There needs to be a commitment to make that the way of one's own personal journey. Failure to do so puts a person in the camp of the second type of people, those who are evil, shallow, and separated from God. *Faithful* is the word that describes the second, the BEING, quality of this equation for happiness.

The June 1990, issue of the *Journal for the Scientific Study of Religion* reported a documented finding that doesn't really surprise me. Research showed that

> *People who believe strongly in their religion have lower personal distress levels than those people who profess a weak belief. Thus there's a strong link between our belief system and the measure of well-being we experience.*

people who believe strongly in their religion have lower personal distress levels than those people who profess a weak belief. Thus there's a strong link between our belief system and the measure of well-being we experience. When the belief is right, the outcome will be a step closer to being happy.

The third leg of this stool is DOING. What must a person "do" in order to have this experience of deep and life-sustaining happiness? This is a simple psalm, as I said earlier, and the answer to that question is both simple and clear. Our happiness is a function of being obedient to the directives of the torah, which we have committed ourselves to follow. In verse two we read, "they find joy in obeying the Law of the Lord, they study it day and night," which is to say that they lose themselves in a lifelong pursuit of knowing how God directs us to be living.

Someone has noticed that happiness is like a shadow. Run after it and you will never catch it, but keep your face to the sun and it will follow you everywhere. Developing a comprehension of the torah — God's best wisdom on how we ought to live — is like keeping your face to the sun, and will surely lead to the happiness you deserve and desire. It beats the heck out of chasing after elusive forms of a temporary pleasure.

## Conclusion

The world has changed a lot since the days of the psalmists. But the wisdom that inspired their lives is the same today as in their time. Happiness is our common effort, though many spend their lives losing the effort to have what God so much wants to give them.

Let us learn from the psalmist about the simple truth of our life's desire. If we want our lives to be going somewhere instead of nowhere, we must recognize that the pathway to happiness comes by a familiarity with God's ways, a commitment to shape our lives around them, and an obedience to make it happen in the daily routines we keep. There's no other way.

## Bulletin Material

# God's Plan For Your Happiness
# Psalm 1 (A Psalm Of Orientation)

### Notes of the Psalms of Orientation
All the psalms used in worship today and next Sunday are Psalms of Orientation. The function of this type of psalm is to praise and thank God. "I will sing to the Lord as long as I live!" exclaims the psalmist (104:33a). Such religious conviction comes from those who experience life as good, generous, and reliable. The psalms are statements that describe a happy, blessed state in which the speakers are grateful for and confident in the abiding, reliable gifts of life that are longstanding from time past and will endure for time to come.

Generally these psalms represent the viewpoints of those who are already experiencing the richness of life which God has to give. But the sentiment expressed in the Psalms of Orientation also speaks for those who cling with hope to the possibility that God's graciousness will also someday be extended to them. "My soul melts away for sorrow; strengthen me according to your word" (119:28). Thus there is a quality of hoped-for justice which may in the present only be partially known, but which will eventually be evident throughout all Creation.

### Hymn No. 1
Psalm 84 (Tune: Aurelia, "The Church's One Foundation")

How lovely is your dwelling, O Lord, the God of Hosts.
We hunger for your presence; In you alone we boast.
Our hearts long for your courtyard, To dwell there all our days.
How blest are those who trust you And live to sing your praise.

The sparrow and the swallow Find safety there and rest.
Within your sheltering presence, They build their young's nest.

15

We place our lives before you, Just as they place their own.
Like them we seek your presence, To make your courts our
home.

How blest are those who seek you, And find your pathway true.
Their hearts walk down your highway, They find their strength
in you.
When passing through deep sorrow, Springs well up from their
tears,
To clothe the land with blessings, To strengthen all their years.
Amen.


**Hymn No. 2**
Psalm 119 (Tune: St. Louis, "O Little Town Of Bethlehem")

Blest are the uncorrupt in heart, Whose ways are right and true,
Who never from your law depart, But ever fly to you.
Blest are those who your word keep, And practice your
commands,
Who with their hearts still seek you, Lord, And serve you with
their hands.

Great hope we find without your law, Thus firm our lives are
bound.
When trials, troubles, hurts arise, In you true life is found.
Then do we sing with deep joy, The honor of your name.
For when your statutes we obey, Our lives are kept from shame.
Amen.


**Hymn No. 3**
Psalm 24 (Tune: Joanna, "Immortal, Invisible, God Only
Wise")

The earth is yours, Lord, and the fullness of all
The world and its people, the great and the small.
For you have established all things on the earth,
All matter, all creatures in this universe.

And who shall ascend to the hill of the Lord?
To stand in God's presence and worship afford?
All those with clean hands and all those with pure hearts
Who give not their living to do evil's arts.

All these will be blest by the hand of the Lord.
Salvation and honor are their sure reward.
How blest are the ones who in life seek your face,
Who long for your presence to sing of your grace.

Then lift up your gates now, come open your doors.
The King of all ages now comes to these shores.
And who is this Royal One, coming to reign?
The King of all glory, forever the same. Amen.

**Call to Worship:**

> **Leader:** Lord, Who may enter your Temple? Who may worship on Zion, your sacred hill?
>
> **People:** A person who obeys God in everything and always does what is right, whose words are true and sincere.
>
> **Leader:** The worship of the Lord is good; it will continue forever.
>
> **People:** The judgments of the Lord are just; they are always fair.
>
> **Leader:** They are more desirable than the finest gold; they are sweeter than the purest honey.
>
> **People:** May our words and our thoughts be acceptable to you, O Lord, my refuge and my redeemer. (Psalm 15:1-2; 19:9-10, 14)

**Call to Confession:**

The proof of God's amazing love is this: while we were sinners Christ died for us. Because we have faith in him, we dare to approach God with confidence. (Romans 5:8, Hebrews 4:16) Let us admit our sins before God.

**Prayer of Confession:** (Unison)
God of compassion, in Jesus Christ we behold your transforming light, yet we live in darkness. Preoccupied with ourselves, we fail to see your work in the world. We speak when we should listen; we act when we should reflect. Empower us to live in your light and to walk in your ways for the sake of him who is the light of the world, Jesus Christ our Lord and Savior. Amen.

**Declaration of Pardon:**
The mercy of the Lord is from everlasting to everlasting. I declare to you, in the name of Jesus Christ, you are forgiven. Amen and amen.

**Hymn of Response:** (Please sing after the organist plays the melody once)
> Lord, great wonders workest Thou! To Thy sway all creatures bow.
> Write Thou deeply in my heart what I am, and what Thou art.

*(Note: The tune for this response is Gott Sei Dank Durch Alle Welt, "Heaven And Earth, And Sea, And Air," Psalm 19)*

# Since He's In Charge, We're In Luck

## Psalm 33:4-5, 8-9, 13-22

**Introduction**

At the turn of the century the storm clouds that had long been gathering in South Africa suddenly broke loose. Britain and the English-speaking South Africans went to war with the Dutch-descended Boers. The British newspaper, *The Morning Post,* offered a young reporter by the name of Winston Churchill the job of chief war correspondent to cover the story. He jumped at the chance. Soon after he arrived in South Africa he was traveling on a troop train when it was captured and he was taken prisoner.

After three weeks he escaped. The first night of his freedom he slept among the empty coal bags of a train. He hid during the day, and then the second night as he traveled he saw the lights of a mining town in the distance. He decided to chance his luck. He knocked on a door and a tall man eyed him with suspicion — until he gave the man his name. "Thank God you've come here," the man in the doorway said. "It is the only house in 20 miles where you would not have been handed over."

What was going on in this event? Was it an accident that a young newspaperman knocked on the only door in the territory where he would be safe? Maybe fate turns over a lucky card once in a statistical long-shot and Churchill just got lucky. Or was there more going on here than simply blind fate playing out her hand? What do you think?

> *Sooner or later we all run up against the metaphysical question of why things happen the way that they do.*

**A**

I'm sure that you also have experienced some events in your life which needed a bigger explanation than simply "it just happened that way." I've had them, too. Sooner or later we all run up against the metaphysical question of why things happen the way that they do. Why did something happen one way instead of another? Many times we can't explain why something did occur or did not occur. But we may well sense that there is more happening than simply fate.

Think of it this way. At one end of a spectrum there exists the possibility that everything is determined. Certain natural laws are in place which regulate and control the course of the planets, the chemical reactions of natural elements, and everything else that is predictable. Those who argue that we live in this kind of a world would say that whatever happens, happens because the Laws of Nature made it happen that way. Combined with that is the design of an Absolute Tyrant who sets in motion every action within Creation, both great and small.

At the other end of the spectrum is the argument of some that nothing is planned. Everything that happens is accidental. Two events may appear to be related in some way, but in actuality they are random happenings that we suppose are connected to each other. But in reality, they are just coincidence.

Neither view seems to quite fit the world which we experience. But there is room for a viewpoint somewhere along that spectrum which suggests that order has been built into the Creation and that living creatures are given a measure of freedom as well. People who believe that God continues to be actively involved in his creation hold to the notion that we are in some way living in partnership with God, exercising co-creative powers to help shape the ultimate outcome of things.

An intercessory prayer for the sake of another is a good example of this kind of partnership involvement with God to effect a particular outcome. There are points in between on this spectrum, to be sure. But the point is that some people resist the fatalistic notion that they are a chance collection of molecules cast out onto an empty stage to dance around for so many years before death overcomes them. That's what faith is about.

*Some people resist the fatalistic notion that they are a chance collection of molecules cast out onto an empty stage to dance around for so many years before death overcomes them. That's what faith is about.*

Now the psalmists and the people of the Bible were people of faith. And people of faith tend *not* to be clustered at either end of the spectrum where the belief is that the world is highly deterministic and highly coincidental. People of faith lean to the belief in a managed universe, watched over by some type of personal force that cares about what happens. People who hold a biblical faith know that Divine Character as God.

It was God who brought the world into being. It was God who called a man named Abram to become the father of the Hebrew nation. It was God who led the Hebrew slaves out of Egypt and through the wilderness. It was God who safely brought the people into a Promised Land where their destiny would be to live as a chosen people. It was God who sent a savior into the world. It was God who sent the Holy Spirit to create a community of people whose lives were focused on the transforming power of the resurrection of Jesus, and they became the Christian Church. God was at work throughout the ages to make certain things happen.

I suppose you can embrace a faith that believes that God controls the big things that happen, like saving an entire neighborhood from being burned up in a wildcat fire, and not pay much attention to the little things that go on in the world. Such an idea wasn't good enough for the people of the Bible. The psalmists in particular believed that God watched over every little thing, and could intervene for the well-being of any one of us at any time when it fit his purposes to do so. This is what Richard Lovelace of Gordon-Conwell Seminary calls "a strong faith in the divine architecture of human lives."

I'm speaking now of the individual as well as the universal dimension of God's providential relationship with his world. Galileo, the seventeenth century Italian astronomer and mathematician, saw the mystery of this, noting that the "sun, which has all those planets revolving around it and dependent on it for their order function, can ripen a bunch of grapes as if it had nothing else in the world to do." In the same way God can create and sustain a universe that is still too big for us to see, and at the same time keep you and me safe from danger and guided in a way that accomplishes his purposes.

> *The psalmists in particular believed that God watched over every little thing, and could intervene for the well-being of any one of us at any time when it fit his purpose.*

## B

How does God tend to the little things, the details that are the stuff of our lives? I can tell you of three distinct ways in which God provides for people of faith because of his concern for us and for the world. Some who have experienced a purposive dimension in their lives have experienced a sense of being spared from some crisis or disaster. Winston Churchill felt he received special consideration that night in South Africa when he literally came to the only possible door that was safe for him. When the earthquake that struck in southern

California on Martin Luther King Jr. Day, 1994, collapsed an entire floor of an apartment building, some people who should have been killed crawled out from the wreckage without a scratch. They were spared.

Another way that the providence of God is known to us is when we believe we have been led to a new place. Alex Haley is one who testifies to this. He spent 12 years of research and writing before he finished his history-making book *Roots*. In retrospect Haley believes it was more than his own perseverance that got the book finished. "However it sounds," he says, "it was one of those things that God in his infinite wisdom and in his time and way decided should happen. I feel I'm a conduit through which this is happening. It was just something that was meant to be. I say this because there were so many things that had to happen over which I had no control. And if any one thing hadn't happened, then this could not have come together."

> *The marvelous thing about the psalmists who faced great hardships is that they didn't lose their faith. Some days I'm sure they came close.*

Probably the greatest way that we experience the Providence of God is in a third capacity. We experience him as One who sustains us in our travails and upholds us when the floor gives way beneath us. The psalmists and many others in the biblical story came to rely upon the strong arms of the Lord reaching out to keep us close to him when the world around seemed to be coming unglued. "Pollyanna" is not a good word to describe the outlook of the psalmists, who knew great personal and national tragedy. Many are the passages which bemoan the terrible state of affairs they faced. We're going to talk more about this in the second type of psalms — the Psalms of Disorientation.

The marvelous thing about the psalmists who faced great hardships is that they didn't lose their faith. Some days I'm sure they came close. But they had a deep and abiding confidence in the ways of the Lord to know that *no matter how*

23

*great the catastrophe, God's power to sustain them through it would not let them down.*

Many of you have testified to me the same thing over the years. Some of you have lost to death a spouse or parent or good friend. You've known

> *Like the psalmists, we are a people of faith, and we trust that God is at work behind the scenes managing the course of things so that the story will come out right.*

the deep sadness of such a loss, yet you've shared with me a faith that shouldered the loss because you knew that God hadn't given up on you. Some have known a lingering illness and pain; but despite the endless suffering that brought, you have pointed instead to an even stronger experience of God's upholding you through the worst of it.

## Conclusion

That's why we're in luck. Suffering and sadness will always be with us. And if we were left to ourselves, such tragedies could do us in. But like the psalmists, we are a people of faith, and we trust that God is at work behind the scenes managing the course of things so that the story will come out right. For now we may be hurting. But we're still in good shape because this is still God's world and he is "working together for good with those who are called according to his purpose" (Romans 8:28). Whether we experience God as sparing us from harm, or leading us to some special understanding or event or person, or keeping us strong when the forces of evil are overpowering us, God is still in charge.

# Since He's In Charge, We're In Luck
## Psalm 33:4-5, 8-9, 13-22 (A Psalm Of Orientation)

**Notes of the Psalms of Orientation**

"Life, as reflected in these psalms, is not troubled or threatened, but is seen as the well-ordered world intended by God. They approximate a 'no surprise world,' and consequently a world of 'no fear.' They affirm that the world is a well-ordered, reliable, and life-giving system, because God has ordained it that way and continues to preside effectively over the process." They give expression "to the reality that God is trustworthy and reliable, and to the decision to stake life on this particular God." Even if God's goodness is not completely experienced at the present time in life, the psalmist asserts a measure of assurance "acknowledging that the creation of God has not been fully completed, but this community waits with confidence." (quotations from Walter Brueggeman, *The Message of the Psalms*)

**Hymn No. 1**
Psalm 145 (Tune: National Hymn, "God Of Our Fathers")

We will extol your praise, our God and King,
 And bless your name forever, without end.
With each new day your constant praise we'll sing
 And raise our voices in the great amen.

Great are you, Lord, and greatly to be praised.
 Your ways unsearchable, your wisdom true.
Each generation learning of your ways
 Shall sing unending psalms of thanks to you.

So now we sing your kingdom's glorious reign,
 Telling of purpose that sustains the earth,

That all the people of this world's domain
Shall come to know the splendor of new birth.

So bring your kingdom, bring your vict'ry, Lord.
The day your people long to see appear;
A time of peace without a need for sword,
A reign where generations have no fear. Amen.

**Hymn No. 2**
Psalm 8 (Tune: Winchester Old, "God Is Our Refuge And
Our Strength")

O Lord, our God, how excellent, How glorious is your name.
Your majesty surrounds the earth, And children sing your
fame.

The heavens shout your handiwork; We stand beneath in awe,
To think the one who made all things, Should care for us at all.

Yet you have made us less than gods, Surpassing all but you.
With heart and mind, with strength and will, To search for
what is true.

O Lord, our God, how excellent, How glorious is your name,
Majestic in your holiness. We sing and praise your fame.
Amen.

**Hymn No. 3**
Psalm 104 (Tune: Hymn to Joy, "Joyful, Joyful, We Adore
Thee")

Bless the Lord with all my being, Lord my God, you have such
might.
Cloaked with honor, grand and glorious, You are clothed with
purest light
Stretching out the heavens like tent cloth, You are chambered
on the deep
Riding on the wings of windstorm, Flame and fire your bidding keep.

Lord, you laid the earth's foundation, That it would be always sound.
By the word of your commanding, You set forth each ocean's bound.
Springs gush forth at your own bidding, Giving drink to every field.
Birds and beast and all your creatures, In that coolness find thirst healed.

Grass you cause to grow for cattle, Plants for us to cultivate.
Food you bring forth from our labor, Wine for joy and bread for plate.
Trees you give the birds for shelter, Mountain rock and cave for beast.
Sun and moon both mark the seasons, In their light we work and feast.

Lord, how great are all your workings, Wisdom marks them through and through.
All the earth is your possession, Great and small belong to you.
Food you give in each due season, At your hand came all good things.
By your Spirit you create us; Lord, your breath renewal brings.
Amen.


## Call to Worship

**Leader:** Happy are those who have reverence for the Lord, who live by his commands.

**People:** Trust in the Lord and do good; live in the land and be safe.

**Leader:** Seek your happiness in the Lord and he will give you your heart's desire.

**People:** Give yourself to the Lord; trust in him and he will help you. He will make your righteousness shine like the noonday sun.

(Psalm 128:1; 37:3-6)

27

**Call to Confession:**
The Lord is near to the brokenhearted, and saves those who are crushed in spirit (Psalm 34:18). Let us admit our sins before God.

**Prayer of Confession:** (Unison)
Eternal God, our judge and redeemer, we confess that we have tried to hide from you, for we have done wrong. We have lived for ourselves and turned from our neighbors. We have refused to bear the troubles of others. We have ignored the pain of the world, and passed by the hungry, the poor, and the oppressed. O God, in your great mercy forgive our sin and free us from selfishness, that we may choose your will and obey your commandments; through Jesus Christ our Savior. Amen.

**Declaration of Pardon:**
May the God of mercy who forgives you all your sins strengthen you in all goodness, and by the power of the Holy Spirit keep you in eternal life. Amen and amen.

**Hymn of Response:** (Please sing after the organist plays the melody once)
> O God, Our Help in ages past, our hope for years to come,
> Our shelter from the stormy blast and our eternal home.
> Amen.

# When God
# Is The Problem

## Psalm 13

**Introduction**

During Lent we are focusing our biblical attention almost
exclusively on the passages from the psalms, allowing their
themes and their spirit to rise up and identify themselves to
us. Today we are continuing to gain a greater familiarity with
these conversations from the heart. Through song and read-
ing and spoken word the religiosity of the psalmists of old is
speaking to us today.

**A**

For the first two Sundays in Lent our attention was on
what Old Testament professor Walter Brueggeman called
Psalms of Orientation. The reason they're called that is because they hold a definite set of presuppositions about life and
about God which consistently come through. Two of those
fundamental presuppositions
are key: Happiness in life is
directly correlated with living
in harmony with God's Will;
and second, pursuing Wis-
dom is the way to learn

*The Psalms of Disorienta-
tion are written from the
starting point that bad things
happen not just to bad people, but to good people also.*

about God's Will. The "good" person, these psalmists presumed, would naturally and diligently seek to know and live by the will of the Lord.

Today and next Sunday we are looking at another large section of the psalms which *challenges* those notions. In contrast to the Psalms of Orientation, which start with the assumption that there is an underlying goodness in the world, the various Psalms of Disorientation are written from the experience of those for whom that proved NOT to be true. The Psalms of Disorientation are written from the starting point that bad things happen not just to bad people, but to good people also. Sometimes people suffer when they don't deserve it.

*Another is saying, "I take good care of my body; why should I be a victim of muscular dystrophy?"*

How nice it is when we live inside the circle — where the good things of life reside and can be enjoyed. And how uncomfortable are those who cry out in pain and bitterness that their lives are being lived out "outside" the circle and they don't deserve this. Their lives are in some sort of crisis from which they need to be delivered. That crisis could be serious illness, or militant enemies threatening at the borders, or a bad marriage, or children who turn out to be an embarrassment, or gossipy neighbors, or any of a number of things. The issue for them is "This shouldn't be happening to me!"

I know there are people sitting in this sanctuary today who are saying the same thing. "After 27 years of faithful service to my company it isn't fair that I am being retired early and against my wishes." Another is saying, "I take good care of my body; why should I be a victim of muscular dystrophy?" Another, whose retirement years ought to be enjoyable, lives in perpetual disillusionment because the children will have nothing to do with their parents. And the list goes on at great length.

You remember our former attorney general, Ed Meese. He had a memorable way of putting it. Meese liked to recall the advice of the man who preceded him in that office, William

French Smith, who advised Ed Meese that there would be days in this position when he would feel like the javelin competitor who won the coin toss and elected to receive. Some people go through much of their lives in resentment because they are undeservedly living outside the circle, and they don't like it one bit. These people (like all of us if we are brave enough to admit it) have made an implicit bargain with God that if I am honest and caring and a good citizen and a good neighbor and a hard worker, then I deserve a pretty fair measure of good things coming my way.

Most of the time we can get through life without any real challenge to that bargain we've made with God. Most of the time things work out pretty well. Sure, there are rocky places along the path, and once in a while I stub my toe on a rocky outgrowth. But I recover, pick myself up, and keep on living.

> *With a bleeding spirit and a bruised soul we plaintively argue, "I'm keeping MY part of the bargain. Why isn't God keeping his?"*

But some of us don't just stub our toe. We do more than fall down and bruise our elbow. Some of us fall so badly that we can't seem to get back up. And I'm thinking that there are more than just a few people in this sanctuary today who have fallen badly at some point in their life and seriously wondered if they could get back up.

And as bad as the fall was, the even greater hardship than the fall is that our implicit bargain with God was seriously challenged. With a bleeding spirit and a bruised soul we plaintively argue, "I'm keeping MY part of the bargain. Why isn't God keeping his?"

Might you not say along with the psalmist, "How long, O Lord? Will you forget me forever? How long will you hide your face from me? How long must I bear pain in my soul, and have sorrow in my heart all day long? How long shall my enemy be exalted over me?" (vv. 1-2).

31

The real problem that some of us have to live with is not just that life has turned sour, but that life has turned sour and God has forgotten about us.

**B**

What are we to do when it hits us like a two-by-four on the side of the head that God has turned his back on us? You know what some people do. They become very bitter. If they let all their anger out at once they'd explode, so they let it out in constant, belligerent shots fired at everybody for just about everything. They're the "skunks" of this world who make a big stink about everything.

Other people withdraw into themselves. They may become depressed. They may become apathetic. They certainly turn their backs on religion, for that has been a big part of the problem: they trusted God, and God let them down. These people express their anger like "turtles" — quietly but equally effectively.

The psalmist isn't bitter. He isn't withdrawn and pessimistic. Instead he renews his trust in the Lord, the same God who seems to have let him down. There's a simple truth here, and it's a gold mine of spiritual strength when we discover it for ourselves. *Even when God is the problem, God is also the solution. So keep trusting in God, and count on him to deliver you.*

> *Even when God is the problem, God is also the solution. So keep trusting in God, and count on him to deliver you.*

**Conclusion**

Our tendency when we're angry at God and believe he has forgotten about us is to wallow around in our self-pity and become absorbed in our troubles. But that's not the helpful way to go. The better way is the way of faith. The better way is to keep our focus on God and not give up on him. For he hasn't really given up on you. He is still the source of your deliverance and your salvation.

# When God Is The Problem
## Psalm 13 (A Psalm Of Disorientation)

### Notes of the Psalms of Disorientation

We'd like to think that everything is managed and under control; that things inevitably come out right in the end. We cling to the hope that enough knowledge and good intentions will eliminate the darkness in our lives. Unfortunately, the darkness has a remarkable resiliency.

We know that not everything does come out right in the end. Good intentions sometimes get us in trouble. Innocent people sometimes experience great hardships. Sometimes we are victims of other people's mistakes and sins.

These Psalms of Disorientation recognize the unfairness in life and the extreme hardship that some deserving people unavoidably suffer. With amazing candor the people of Old Testament times felt free to cry out in pain and sorrow, to vent their anger at God and anyone else, and to argue their case in the highest courts of the Lord. And while there often was no possibility of changing the reality against which they railed, there was healing and comfort that came by "talking out" the problem and knowing that the cry for mercy was heard.

### Hymn No. 1
Psalm 90 (Tune: St. Catherine, "Faith Of Our Fathers")

Lord, Thou hast been our dwelling place
    Through the ages of our race;
Before the mountains had their birth
    Or even Thou hadst formed the earth.
From everlasting Thou art God; To everlasting our abode.

O teach Thou us to count our days
    And set our hearts on wisdom's ways;

33

Turn, Lord, to us in our distress.
In pity now Thy servants bless.
Let mercy's dawn dispel our night, And all our day with joy
be bright.

O send the day of joy and light,
For long has been our sorrow's night;
Afflicted through the weary years,
We wait until Thy help appears;
With us and with our sons abide, In us let God be glorified.
Amen.

## Hymn No. 2
Psalm 80 (Tune: Marion, "Rejoice, Ye Pure In Heart")

Hear our cry, O Lord. Now hear us as we pray.
You guide us as a shepherd leads, So keep us in your way.
O come, Lord, come. Restore and save us now.

Enthroned above all worlds, You shine with holy light.
Lord, pour your power upon us all, And save us with your
might.
O come, Lord, come. Restore and save us now.

O Lord, the God of Hosts, Turn not your face away.
Our tears have been both food and drink, Foes mock us night
and day.
O come, Lord, come. Restore and save us now.

O Lord, our God, return. Bring peace into each home.
So let your face shine on us all, Restore us as your own.
O come, Lord, come. Restore and save us now. Amen.

## Hymn No. 3
Psalm 51 (Tune: Evan, "The Lord's My Shepherd")

Have mercy on us, living Lord, Remember not our sin.
According to your steadfast love, Come cleanse us from within.

Our sin and guilt are heavy, Lord, And evil in your sight.
Against you only have we sinned, Your judgment, Lord, is
right.

34

We're born into a guilty world, And sinful in our ways,
Lord, teach us wisdom in our hearts, And lead us all our days.

So come and purify our lives, Our hearts with love redeem.
Restore us to your life-filled ways. Come, Lord, and make us
clean. Amen.

**Call to Worship:**

> **Leader:** God is our Shelter and our Strength, always ready to help in times of trouble.
>
> **People:** So we will not be afraid, even if the earth is shaken and mountains fall into the ocean depths; even if the seas roar and rage, and the hills are shaken by the violence.
>
> **Leader:** There is a river that brings joy to the city of God, to the sacred house of the Most High.
>
> **People:** God is in that city, and it will never be destroyed; at early dawn he will come to its aid.
>
> **Leader:** Nations are terrified, kingdoms are shaken; God thunders and the earth dissolves.
>
> **People:** The Lord Almighty is with us; the God of Jacob is our refuge.
>
> **Leader:** Come and see what the Lord has done. See what amazing things he has done on earth.
>
> (Psalm 46:1-8)

**Call to Confession:**
Our God is a God of justice, waiting to be gracious to you, yearning to have pity on you. Blessed are all who wait on the Lord. In penitence and faith, let us confess our sin to Almighty God.

**Prayer of Confession:** (Unison)
Lord, we feel that we are lost from you in the midst of the changes and challenges facing our church and our own lives. We see dimly ahead of us, due to our lack of faith in you

and in ourselves. Forgive us for having wasted yesterday, for failing to make the most of the opportunities, and for failing to plan to become better followers in the future. Help us not to waste today, but to use wisely the opportunities that come to us for strengthening our faith and for serving you. Guide us to look forward to tomorrow when we shall see, and know and understand, through Christ. Amen.

**Declaration of Pardon:**
Hear the good news! Who is in a position to condemn? Only Christ, and Christ died for us. Christ rose for us. Christ reigns in power for us. Christ prays for us (Romans 8:34). Anyone who is in Christ is a new creation. The old life is gone; a new life has begun (2 Corinthians 5:17). Friends, believe the gospel. In Jesus Christ we are forgiven.

**Hymn of Response:** (Please sing after the organist plays the melody once)
> Did we in our own strength confide, our striving would be losing;
> Were not the right man on our side, the man of God's own choosing.
> Dost ask who that may be? Christ Jesus, it is he, Lord Sabaoth his name,
> From age to age the same, and he must win the battle.

*(Note: The tune for this response is Ein' Feste Burg, "A Mighty Fortress Is Our God," Psalm 46).*

# A Faith I Could No Longer Count On

## Psalm 73:1-7, 13-18

**Introduction**

The seventy-third psalm mirrors the life of faith for every-one who is honest enough to allow his or her faith to be pushed to the limit. It begins with a simple, Sunday School outlook which lifts up the clear virtue of a good God who is good to good people. We all like that sort of thing, and quickly say "Amen" to that.

It doesn't take long at all for the psalmist to "grow up" and realize that the simple theology of a good God smiling on good people doesn't hold much water. Just because that's what Mrs. Gray says in the primary Sunday school class doesn't mean that's the way it is in the real world. No wonder so many children barely make it through a junior high confirmation experience — they're too smart to fall for the trite thinking we sometimes espouse in the name of religion. They know that sometimes good guys come in last. They know you've got to break the rules to get ahead, and sometimes you have to bend a few rules even to get by.

**A**

This psalm is about faith that goes into crisis. We deceive ourselves if we think that faith is some kind of automatic

37

protection from spiritual crisis. People with great measures of faith have faced agonizing periods in their lives when the most important things they believed and hoped for were denied. Having much faith only means that the crisis challenging that faith can be that much more overwhelming. Think of Jesus in the Garden of Gethsemane.

What was the faith crisis of the psalmist? It is one common to many today. He presumed that his goodness and honesty would be the premiums that would regularly pay off nicely in the form of dividends that make life comfortable. But it didn't work out that way. He built his faith upon the notion that good things happen to good people and bad things happen to bad people. But it wasn't happening.

> Christians have been attracted to the psalms for many centuries, and for good reason. They exhibit a stark honesty.

We don't know if this happened over a long period of time, or if he woke up one morning and it hit him. He looked around him and it sunk in that his neighbors were prosperous and satisfied and secure in their lives, and he wasn't. His wicked neighbors were getting along famously. They had the very things that this man lacked, and it made him angry. He was rightly angry for two reasons: HE should be living the good life, and THEY shouldn't!

Listen to his own words: "I was envious of the arrogant; I saw the prosperity of the wicked. For they have no pain; their bodies are sound and sleek. They are not plagued like other people." And then, like a knife that is turned back onto oneself, he despairs, "All in vain I have kept my heart clean and washed my hands in innocence." With bitter resignation he concludes, "For all day long I have been plagued, and am punished every morning" (vv. 3-4, 5b, 13-14).

Christians have been attracted to the psalms for many centuries, and for good reason. They exhibit a stark honesty. Nobody tries to "pretty-up" their faith and make it sound like something that Madison Avenue has gotten hold of. The psalmists tell it like it is. When God has let them down, they say so. When they're getting what they don't deserve, and not getting what they do deserve, they speak up!

Woe to us when we come across those syrupy Christians for whom life is always just wonderful. "Spiritual exhibitionists," that's what they are. Their faith keeps them right up there on the mountaintop, and they never experience the deep valleys, the dark shadows of doubt and fear. They make us feel like we must have gotten our faith at WalMart.

Thank God that the psalmists weren't like that. In this case the faith of the psalmist has been severely trampled on. And he cannot hold back the pain and sadness that he feels.

## B

The crisis of faith which we read about in the seventy-third psalm makes me think of an incident that we hear about from time to time. When there are speedboat races with high-powered and streamlined boats racing across the water at breakneck speeds, the drivers of those boats race them at great risk to themselves. For if there's even a little problem, it can become very big very quickly because of the extremely fast speeds.

> He went into the sanctuary of the Lord, and something happened that made all the difference in the world. He experienced a renewal of mind and spirit that put him back on track once again.

Once in a while we hear about a speedboat racer who experiences some difficulty and is thrown from his boat — maybe a wave hits the boat at a bad angle, maybe a turn was taken too sharply. The driver is ejected and hits the water with great force, propelling him deep below the surface.

In those quick, traumatic moments there is only one thing which the speedboat driver can do to save himself. If he fails to do this, he will surely die. When he has been thrown into the water, he must relax and make no effort to save himself. In that confusing moment, he won't know which way to swim to the surface of the water. He must remain calm and allow the life-saving quality of his life jacket to take over, gently lifting him to the surface and safety.

The psalmist discovered that this same thing works in the life of faith. In the time of crisis, when the old rules don't apply and things don't

> *He sees God among them. And he can no longer be angry and distraught.*

happen the way they're supposed to, the wrong thing to do is to run off in three directions with a burst of energy and greater determination to make it right. No, that would compound the crisis. The thing to do is to take a step back and re-examine the situation. The thing to do is to create the right context to begin to feel the gentle tug of God's hand directing you to the surface and to safety.

Listen once more to the psalmist, to the wisdom that he speaks in the middle of his crisis: "If I had said 'I will walk on this way,' I would have been untrue to the circle of your children. But when I thought how to understand this, it seemed to me a wearisome task until I went into the sanctuary of God; then I perceived their end" (vv. 15-17).

". . . until I went into the sanctuary of God." Something happened in that experience of coming into the presence of God that turned everything around. Before this his thoughts were turned in on themselves. You know what it's like when your mind races and you argue with yourself about why things shouldn't be the way they are. The psalmist was becoming miserable because he couldn't get out of himself.

> *The thing to do is to create the right context to begin to feel the gentle tug of God's hand directing you to the surface and to safety.*

It was at that point that he did a very smart thing. He went into the sanctuary of the Lord, and something happened that made all the difference in the world. He experienced a renewal of mind and spirit that put him back on track once again.

I'm not sure that we typically appreciate the impact it can have on us when we enter into the temple of the Lord. Yes, I realize that our regularity at worship puts us at risk of falling into a routine habit that dulls us to the dynamism of stepping into the presence of God. On the surface of things, it seems innocent enough. We "go to church." We take our seat in the pew (probably the same one we've been sitting in for many years). We expect to see the same faces in the choir. The prayers of the minister sound familiar. The hymnbook we hold as we sing shows the same years of use that our faith has had. On the surface of things, we shouldn't expect much from going to worship.

> Something can happen in our lives which is like stepping out of a dark room into a bright, sunny day.

But how wrong we can be! For in that moment, when faith has the opportunity to become the primary voice we hear, something can happen in our lives which is like stepping out of a dark room into a bright, sunny day. We can come in cross and disturbed, and leave feeling hopeful and inspired again. We probably can't explain what happened to us in the sanctuary, but we are living proof that something happened between God and his people that left a profound impact on some. Meaning has come back into their lives. The resolve is there to put energy into a faltering marriage. Forgiveness begins to bleed into a troubled relationship between a disappointed father and his angry son. It will be different for different people. But it's universally true that miracles happen when God meets his people in the sanctuary of the Lord.

At least two things happened to the psalmist that help us understand the change. When he went into the temple he began to realize once again that God is a just God. It *seems* that the wicked are getting away with murder. But that's not really the case. For God will exercise his just judgment on them, as he will on all of us. Their misdeeds will not go unrecognized and unpunished.

41

The psalmist also experiences a transformation because he has surrounded himself in a sea of faces of fellow pilgrims who bring their same questions and doubts. He knows he is in good company, for they too have had their faith tested and are needing to know that God can deal with them as well. He looks out on the faces of those who have come with him into the sanctuary of the Lord, and in their faces, he sees the tender face of God. Because they are there together, he sees God among them. And he can no longer be angry and distraught.

> *We can't say why good people suffer and the wicked thrive. We can only testify that when God's faithful people come into his presence in the sanctuary of the Lord, the pressing need for an explanation doesn't seem to matter much any more.*

## Conclusion

The psalmist made a life-changing discovery as he went into the temple that day. Others have made it before us, and we can make the same discovery. They have discovered that the only faith they can count on is not one that tries to unravel the mysteries of life with logical explanations, nor one that comes with pat answers to life's most difficult questions. *They have discovered that the only faith they can count on is one which enables them to experience God unencumbered by the need to have logical explanations and pat answers.*

We can't say why good people suffer and the wicked thrive. We can only testify that when God's faithful people come into his presence in the sanctuary of the Lord, the pressing need for an explanation doesn't seem to matter much any more.

# A Faith I Could No Longer Count On
## Psalm 73:1-7, 13-18 (A Psalm Of Disorientation)

### Notes of the Psalms of Disorientation

Although happiness is what we so much want, suffering and pain seem to be so much more common to many people. Deserved or not, their lives are racked with physical and emotional trauma which skews their ability to rejoice and be glad. Taunted by enemies to the point of death (42:10), like sheep blindly being led to the slaughter (44:11), the psalmist questions God's interest in his people. All too often it was difficult if not impossible to be optimistic about anything when the picture looked so dark.

In part the sadness comes from the realization that God is indeed in charge of all things, but somehow his plans have become thwarted. The world as we experience it has broken down and God's will has not yet been fulfilled. But in this we experience a great frustration and anger, directed at a host of "enemies" who keep us from tasting the glorious banquet of God's rule.

### Hymn No. 1
Psalm 22 (Tune: Ellacombe, "I Sing The Mighty Power Of God")

Amid the thronging worshipers The living Lord I bless;
Before my people gathered here, God's name will I confess.
　　Come sing with all who fear the Lord
　　You children of God's grace;
With reverence sound all glory forth And bow before God's
　　face.

The burden of the sorrowful The Lord will not despise;
God has not turned from those who mourn But listens to their
　　cries.

Such goodness makes me join the throng
Where saints this praise proclaim,
And there will I fulfill my vows With those who fear God's name.

Before you, Lord, the proud shall bow, The haughty with their trust.
They cannot keep themselves alive; They too return to dust.
But you, Lord, dwell beyond all time,
Deliverance to proclaim
To generations yet unborn Who shall confess your name.
Amen.

**Hymn No. 2**
Psalm 32 (Tune: Lancashire, "Lead On, O King Eternal")

How blest are those whose great sin Has freely been forgiven.
Whose guilt is wholly covered Before the sight of heaven.
Blest those to whom our Lord God Will not impute their sin,
Whose guilt has been forgiven, Whose heart is true again.

While I kept guilty silence My strength was spent with grief.
Your hand was heavy on me; My life found no relief.
When then I made confession, And hid no sin from you,
When I revealed my own guilt, You gave me life anew. Amen.

**Hymn No. 3**
Psalm 5 (Tune: Melita, "Eternal Father, Strong To Save")

As morning dawns, Lord, hear our cry,
O sovereign God, now hear our sigh.
As first light brings the sun's warm rays,
Accept our sacrifice of praise.
 Before you, Lord, the wicked fall,
 And none shall dwell within your hall.

The proud shall never gain a place,
Nor evil live to see your face.
Your steadfast love shall welcome all,

44

Who seek your house and on you call.
O lead us, Lord, in righteousness,
As through this day your name we bless.

Let all who seek you then rejoice
And sing to you with joyful voice.
Redeemed by God upon his throne,
Our grateful hearts your mercies own.
For you shall bless the righteous, Lord.
Forever be your name adored. Amen.


**Call to Worship:**

    **Leader:** Praise God with shouts of joy, all people! Sing to the glory of his name; offer him glorious praise!

    **People:** Say to God, "How wonderful are the things you do! Your power is so great that your enemies bow down in fear before you. Everyone on earth worships you; they sing praises to your name."

    **Leader:** Come and listen, all who honor God, and I will tell you what he has done for me. I cried to him for help. I praised him with songs. If I had ignored my sins the Lord would not have listened to me. But God has indeed heard me; he has listened to my prayer.

    **People:** I praise God because he did not reject my prayer, or keep back his constant love from me.
                     (Psalm 66:1-4, 16-20)


**Call to Confession:**
If anyone sins we have someone who pleads with the Father on our behalf — Jesus Christ, the righteous one. And Christ himself is the means by which our sins are forgiven; and not our sins only, but also the sins of everyone (1 John 2:1-2). Let us confess our sins before God and one another.

**Prayer of Confession:** (Unison)
Merciful God, we confess that we have often failed to be an obedient church. We have not done your will; we have broken your law; we have rebelled against your love. We have not loved our neighbors, and have refused to hear the cry of the needy. Forgive us, we pray, and free us for joyful obedience; through Jesus Christ our Lord. Amen.

**Declaration of Pardon:**
The saying is sure and worthy of full acceptance, that Christ Jesus came into the world to save sinners. Christ himself bore our sins in his body on the cross, so that, free from sin, we might live for righteousness. In the name of Jesus Christ, we are forgiven! Since God has forgiven us in Christ, let us forgive one another. The peace of our Lord Jesus Christ be with you all. Amen and amen.

**Hymn of Response:** (Please sing after the organist plays the melody once)
> Goodness and mercy all my life shall surely follow me;
> And in God's house forevermore my dwelling place shall
> be. Amen.

*(Note: The tune for this response is Evan, "The Lord's My Shepherd," Psalm 23)*

# Confidence
# To Spare

## Psalm 27:1-6, 13-14

**Introduction**

A year and a half ago as I was greeting people at the rear door of the sanctuary following worship one Sunday, I talked with a visitor to worship that day. Standing behind this visitor was Mabel Yark. Mabel is one of my favorite people; she's a favorite with many people. Now you need to know that I have the kind of relationship with Mabel that I could say this to the visitor that day. I introduced him to Mabel and I invited him to guess Mabel's age. I know Mabel would not be offended. He thought a moment then he said, "Maybe about 80." Mabel smiled and said, "On my next birthday I'm going to be 100!"

I thought to myself that was just wonderful. She didn't say, "I'm 99." She said, "I'm going to be 100." That's confidence.

Mabel is without question a cheerful and caring and appreciative woman. In all my years I've never met anyone like Mabel. She's never blue or upset about something. She never complains. She's a good example of what I'm talking about today, for she illustrates the human attribute of confidence. She is a good demonstration of my point that confidence is a very valuable attribute to have in life, because it raises the level of the quality of your life. When you have confidence, just about everything else is good. Even a bad day in the life of a person who has a high level of confidence is measurably better than a very good day in the life of a person with only a moderate amount of confidence.

> *Even a bad day in the life of a person who has a high level of confidence is measurably better than a very good day in the life of a person with only a moderate amount of confidence.*

**A**

Let me say a quick word about what confidence isn't. Confidence isn't wishful thinking. When you want to have something but don't already have it, anything that looks like confidence is just a put-on. The Reverend Glendon Harris tells about an experience he had once when visiting an elderly woman in a nursing home. She and the others living there were celebrating her 100th birthday. She was as alert as you or I, and enjoyed every moment of it. A newspaper reporter at the party asked her, "Do you have any children?" She responded without any hesitation, "Not yet."

That was a cute thing to say in light of the occasion for the question. But I don't put it in quite the same league as Mabel Yark's response. For the 100-year-old woman without children really doesn't have much of a chance of ever giving birth. It's a pipe-dream to think she might. But there was a good chance that Mabel Yark would celebrate her 100th birthday. In fact, she is enjoying good health in the 101st year of her life!

Confidence. I submit to you that the attitude of confidence is a good reason that Mabel has done so well for so long. Confidence in many ways is STRENGTH. It's the state of mind that operates on firm footing, and consistently "leans into something." Confidence grows out of the courage to be and the desire to become. Confidence enables a person to take initiative. And as Mabel Yark so nicely illustrates, confidence is grounded in reality. Confidence is central to your outlook in life. When you have confidence you have a springboard to do many fine things. That's because your life has focus. And without confidence, even the little things become difficult.

> *To say it bluntly, the psalmist is no longer stuck in his problem.*

Carl Wallenda, the famous circus performer, was killed in the mid-1980s in a tragic fall from the high wire. His name is associated with dangerous tightrope walking, and for years people have been amazed at his family's skill and courage to walk on a rope high above the ground. The news of his death by falling from a tightrope stunned us all.

His widow reported later that for three months before the accident, all he had been thinking about was falling. He was apparently putting all his energy into *not falling* instead of into walking the tightrope. Just as a surplus of confidence can help a person to achieve great heights, the loss of confidence can produce failure and tragedy in any area of life.

**B**

Today our scripture text is from Psalm 27, and this psalm exudes confidence. It is one of many psalms of new orientation — the third and final type of psalm we're looking at in this Lenten series. Psalm 27 raises the subject of religious confidence, so today we'll talk about what it is and how you can get it. Religious confidence is something that we all need and I believe you'll want as you seek to grow in your faith. All people with a deep faith have displayed a high degree of religious confidence. Those psalmists who composed psalms of new orientation had religious confidence. Jesus, coming into Jerusalem in the final week of his life to be crowned with the crown of glory, showed great religious confidence. As followers of his, we can have it, too.

First, what is religious confidence? I've already been suggesting that confidence is the frame of mind that comes from already having a good measure of something, and the strong likelihood that you may soon have even more of it. A good synonym is expectation, as long as that expectation is grounded in reality. Wishful thinking doesn't count.

Religious confidence is similar to this. Religious confidence is the frame of mind that God wants to give us all the things that we need for our faith to thrive and grow. Remember the old gospel spiritual called "Standing On The Promises Of God." As the title suggests, when we're standing on the promises of the Lord

> *When faith is a part of the story then there's more than just what is obvious.*

we can live with confidence that our needs will be met.

Now, how do we get it? Here the psalms of new orientation can guide us. They speak from a three-point position that I will combine into one sentence. Listen carefully. *"Despite the present hardships in your life ... things are not as they seem ... so you can live boldly with your Lord."*

Let's take them one at a time. *"Despite the present hardships in your life ... "* You know what hardships in life are about and I don't need to belabor it. The psalmists knew the full range of hardships that we still experience today. And bless them, they were brash enough to speak them.

But there's something different about voicing the hardships in the psalms of new orientation from voicing those same hardships in the psalms of disorientation. When the psalmists cried out in the psalms of disorientation, they were angry with God; they resented how God was treating them; they felt punished and vulnerable. But now it's different in the psalms of new orientation.

> *Now the psalmist has come to terms with the hardship and made peace with his problem.*

For now the psalmist has come to terms with the hardship and made peace with his problem. Now there's an evident sense of acceptance of the

50

dilemma, and a willingness to move beyond it. To say it bluntly, the psalmist is no longer stuck in his problem.

*"Despite the present hardship ... things are not as they seem ..."* That's the second part, things are not as they seem. The stories of the second World War continue to have a great impact on us, a power that 50 years later we might not have imagined. The recent award-winning film *Schindler's List* proves once again that the faith of some people in the midst of a great international tragedy touches us deeply. Another true story out of that era came from a group of nameless people who were being hunted by the Nazis, and persecuted if they were found. Some of these people took refuge for a prolonged period of time in a dark and cold underground bunker. For many months it was as if the earth had swallowed them up. After the war ended these words were found written boldly on the wall of that bunker.

*I believe in the sun, even if it does not shine.*
*I believe in God, even if he is silent.*
*I believe in love, even if it is hidden.*

*"Despite the present hardships ... things are not as they seem ... so I will live boldly with my Lord."* Under normal circumstances we take our cues for living from the context of our lives. When we've just won the lottery, we feel on top of the world. (I'm not speaking from personal experience here.) When life throws us a curve ball, it can knock us out. But living in faith automatically puts us into something other than normal circumstances. For with faith we can be experiencing some hardship and yet know that things are not as they seem. Said another way, when faith is a part of the story then there's more than just what is obvious.

*"Despite the present hardship ... things are not as they seem ... so I will live boldly with my Lord."*

So with that understanding, we can then take the next step and dare to live boldly, trusting that God is still with us every step of the way. Rosalind Russell was a great testimony to that. She typically played sophisticated and witty career-women in many motion pictures, and displayed memorable talent on the Broadway stage. But perhaps her greatest triumph was the battle she waged in her fight against cancer and arthritis. After her death this poem was found on a slip of paper tucked into her prayer book. For her it was a beacon light calling her to keep on living with the faith that had carried her so far.

> *Trust Him when dark doubts assail thee. Trust him when your faith is small.*
> *Trust Him when simply to trust Him is the hardest thing of all.*

## Conclusion

This three-part sentence of mine (which actually comes from the formula for living put forth by the psalmists of new orientation) is no magic incantation. It is simply the tried and true wisdom of many great people of faith. And when you make it your creed for living, a statement that comes from your heart, it will give you religious confidence to face anything — with confidence to spare.

*"Despite the present hardship . . . things are not as they seem . . . so I will live boldly with my Lord."*

## Confidence To Spare
## Psalm 27:1-6, 13-14 (A Psalm Of New Orientation)

### Notes of the Psalms of New Orientation

There is a third type of psalm to which we now turn. They are the psalms of new orientation. These psalms bear witness to the surprising gift of new life just when none had been expected. The new orientation is not a return to the old stable orientation, for there is no such going back. Rather, the speaker and the community of faith are often surprised by grace, when there emerges in present life a new possibility that is inexplicable and can only be understood as the goodness of God breaking into the situation. "I will extol you, O Lord, for you have drawn me up, and did not let my foes rejoice over me" (30:1). We do not know how such a newness happens any more than we know how a dead person is raised to new life, how a leper is cleansed, or how a blind person can see. But he now raises his voice in ecstasy and testifies in amazement and gratitude that life is somehow new!

### Hymn No. 1
Psalm 46 (Tune: Azmon, "O For A Thousand Tongues To Sing")

> Come praise the Lord with all our lives,
>    Sing thanks and praise each day.
> No other one is worth our hope,
>    For God alone can save.
>
> How blest are those who hope in you,
>    Creator of all things.
> You heal the sick, you feed the poor,
>    Your presence justice brings.

The blind find sight, the fallen hope,
 You set the prisoner free.
You give the homeless living space,
 But fell the proud like trees.

Your reign, O Lord, will never end.
 How can we count its days?
All generations young and old
 Shall live to sing your praise. Amen.

## Hymn No. 2
Psalm 91 (Tune: St. Anne, "O God, Our Help In Ages Past")

All those who dwell in God's cool shade, Cast by the Rock
 most high,
Sing "Lord, my refuge and my rock, On you I will rely."

There is no terror morn or night, No weapon in the day,
Nor crisis rising like the sun, To burn our life away.

Because we call the Lord our God, No evil shall befall,
Our lives, our homes, our every breath; God watches over all.

Because we hold to you in love, You hold us stronger still;
You shower us with life and strength; Salvation is your will.
 Amen.

## Hymn No. 3
Psalm 97 (Tune: Irby, "Once In Royal David's City")

To our God, divine creator, To our Christ the living Son,
To the Spirit, God's own presence, Ever three yet ever One;
 Holy One, to you forever,
 Let all thanks and praise be sung.

All the heavens proclaim your power. All the people praise
 your name.
Those who worship empty idols Boasting still, are put to shame.
 Righteous are your judgments ever,
 Those who boast are put to shame. Amen.

**Call to Worship:**
> **Leader:** Great is the Lord and greatly to be praised in the city of our God.
> **People:** His holy mountain is the joy of all the earth; Mount Zion is the city of a great King.
> **Leader:** We ponder your steadfast love, O God, in the midst of your temple.
> **People:** Your name, O God, like your praise, reaches to the ends of the earth. Your right hand is filled with victory.
> **Leader:** Let Mount Zion be glad, let the towns of Judah rejoice because of your judgments. People of God, walk around Zion and count its towers, take notice of the walls and examine the fortresses, so that you may tell the next generation —
> **People:** "This God is our God forever and ever. He will lead us for all time to come."
> (Psalm 48:1-2, 9-10, 12-14)

**Call to Confession:**
Since we have a great high priest who has passed through the heavens, Jesus, the Son of God, let us with confidence draw near to the throne of grace, that we may receive mercy and find grace to help us in time of need (Hebrews 4:14, 16). Let us ask God to forgive us.

**Prayer of Confession: (Unison)**
Gracious God, you continue to pour out the Holy Spirit on all of humanity, but too often we hold back the Spirit with our sinful ways. We are a selfish and self-indulgent people. You call us to minister to the needs of our brothers and sisters, yet we point our fingers at one another and gossip. We are timid disciples who walk past your children, blinding ourselves to hunger and homelessness. O God, although we are unworthy of your love and care, guide us in the acceptance of opportunities for joyful service. Amen.

55

**Declaration of Pardon:**
In the past you were spiritually dead because of your disobe-dience and sins. But God's mercy is so abundant, and his love for us is so great that while we were spiritually dead in our disobedience he brought us to life with Christ. It is by God's grace that you have been saved through faith. This is not the result of your own efforts, but God's gift, so that no one can boast about it. Amen and amen. (Ephesians 2:1, 4-5, 8-9)

**Hymn of Response:** (Please sing after the organist plays the melody once)
> Eternal are Thy mercies, Lord; Eternal truth attends Thy word. Alleluia! Alleluia!
> Thy praise shall sound from shore to shore, Till suns shall rise and set no more, Alleluia! Alleluia!
> Alleluia! Alleluia! Alleluia! Alleluia! Amen.

*(Note: The tune for this response is Lasst Uns Erfreuen, "From All That Dwell Below The Skies," Psalm 117)*

# Joy Comes
# In The Morning

## Psalm 30:1-5, 11-12

### Introduction

The psalmists of long ago discovered a great truth that poured through in much of what they said and wrote. They discovered that things do not always stay the same, that where once there was trouble and sadness, something can happen that changes trial into triumph. They discovered that when they live in relationship with God, he can surprise us with a stroke of grace, a transformation of circumstances and attitudes that is beyond our ability to comprehend. They discovered that "weeping may linger for the night, but joy comes with the morning."

### A

Jesus certainly must have realized when he met with his disciples in the Upper Room, only hours before he would be apprehended by the temple guard, taken into custody, questioned, ridiculed, and then sentenced to die, that agony and deep personal pain awaited him. Yet when

> *The tears which may flow in the night will give way to joy when it comes in the morning!*

57

he spoke to them the many words from his heart, he spoke not of tragedy and doom but of hope and promise and joy. One of the things that Jesus told them was: "I am telling you the truth: you will cry and weep, but the world will be glad; you will be sad, but your sadness will turn into gladness" (John 16:20). This, from a man who was about to be tortured and die! Again he said, "I have said these things to you so that my joy may be in you, and that your joy may be complete" (John 15:11).

Jesus understood a great mystery of the faith which the psalmists of old also understood, and which he shared with his disciples in the Upper Room: The tears which may flow in the night will give way to joy when it comes in the morning!

The hope of Jesus for the future stands in stark contrast to the terrible outbreak of those women who watched Jesus hanging so helplessly on the cross for the several hours that it took him to die. He was a victim of falsehood and of hatred, which only added to the searing pain of their grief. The good which he did, the salvation of which he spoke, seemed all but forgotten as he hung there to die.

His removal from the cross did not end their grief, for it continued long into the night, throughout the next day, and through that second night. So intense was their grief that they arose early on the first day of the week, when the Sabbath observance was over, and went to the tomb where Jesus had been buried.

*The story of tears becoming sighs of gladness, of darkness giving way to light, became commonplace in the early Church as well.*

And when they arrived, just as the darkness was giving way to the first light of the new day, they could hardly believe what they were seeing. With great joy in their hearts they ran to find the other disciples and tell them the good news also, that their Lord who had been so brutally killed two days before and laid in a tomb was no longer there. His grave clothes remained behind, but the body was gone! Tears of sadness gave way to expectant stories of joy.

This story of tears becoming sighs of gladness, of darkness giving way to light, became commonplace in the early Church as well. Sadness was replaced with jubilation whenever the mystery of God's transforming grace broke into doubt-filled and disheartened lives. So profound was the characteristic of a new joy among them that author Frederic Farrar, in his book *Christ in Art*, says this: "Few facts are more striking in the history of early Christianity than that its records are so largely borrowed from the dark, subterranean places where martyrs were buried, and the persecuted took refuge, yet all their emblems were emblems of gladness."

The apostle Paul heralded this kind of thinking, and stirred within the early Church this important realization. On more than one occasion Paul was a prisoner. Fortunately for us we still retain his writings from those places of imprisonment, and we can discover for ourselves that confinement inside stone walls did not hold down the spirit. For time and again he speaks with joy about what the Lord is doing in him and through him. Any tears of the night are soon gone when the new day brings with it the transforming hope of new life.

**B**

Sometimes it is challenging circumstances and difficult people who bring tears to our eyes in the dark night of our travail. Sometimes we become victims of an illness or of a relationship or a decision made by others who don't even know us which creates heartache — for a month, or a year, or longer. What do we do about that? Can we expect joy to come in the morning when our night has been stained by tears?

*The gift of joy is ours for the taking. That's what Easter is about.*

As Christians with a resurrection faith, we can. For the external conditions of our lives do not need to infect and destroy the internal convictions of our lives without our consent. The gift of joy is ours for the taking. That's what Easter is about.

Not long ago Dr. Hugh Crocker was speaking to a group in Pittsburgh. He was given this opportunity to speak, as were the others that day, because he had experienced some challenge in life which forced him to assess his faith. Crocker told his listeners of his life experiences over the past ten years — how he was nearly killed in a terrible automobile accident. Then, in a totally unrelated turn of events, he talked of his current battle with Parkinson's Disease.

Dr. Crocker wasn't looking for sympathy. Quite the opposite. The point of his story was spoken in these words: "I am determined that no human limitation shall ever strip me of my joy." He had discovered through faith what others have known before him, that joy is the experience of the presence of God lifting us to victory even in the midst of our suffering.

It's always very gratifying when young people who are pressed up against the stern realities of life can also discover that with the transforming intervention of a gracious God, the story can come out differently. I'm thinking of a group of high school young people who invested themselves in a major way to plan and create a float for the homecoming festivities of their school. It took months of preparation and three days of continuous work to complete the job, but at last it was done and ready to be shown.

But in the dark of night, vandals came around and set fire to the float, burning it right down to the trailer upon which it was riding.

The incident was upsetting to many in the school, but especially to those who had poured their hearts and souls into the project. They were angry and they wanted to get even with whoever had done such a terrible thing.

Several in the group who worked on the float had been active in their church youth fellowship, and they persuaded the others to go with them to talk to their minister about this and ask him what they should do. They all sat down together, and after some discussion, they concluded that in spite of the pain and ugliness which are part of the reality of life, they could salvage something good from this traumatizing experience.

The young people left the church and went into a wooded area to gather as much greenery as they could carry. They cut pine branches and picked plants and low-lying shrubbery, and arranged it on the charred remains of the float. They wanted to say to their classmates and everyone else that even in the face of evil and destruction, there is good to be found. They wanted their sense of hope to speak louder than the voices of maliciousness and harm.

The following morning the long parade of floats passed before the crowds gathered for the homecoming events. And when the

> *They learned to keep hoping even in the face of hopelessness.*

awards were announced, the burned float covered with fresh greens won second place!

It's wonderful that this unusual float, which only a few hours before looked like trash, was recognized as a prize entry. Their message of hope and new life did indeed speak to the ugliness of their disaster. But that's not the best thing about this incident. The really important thing is that these young people learned something about picking themselves up and making the best of a bad situation. They learned to keep hoping even in the face of hopelessness. They learned that the spirit of love and forgiveness is mightier than bitterness. They learned that even though tears may flow in the night, joy comes in the morning, and a new day has begun.

**Conclusion**

"Joy is to feel the wonder of being alive," said Victor Golancz. Joy was the experience of those first disciples on Easter morning as the tears of night were brushed away. It is the experience of any of us who encounter the power of darkness and death, in whatever spiritual and physical and emotional form we meet it.

"Let us then," in the words of Saint Francis of Assisi, "leave sadness to the devil and his angels. As for us Christians, what can we be but rejoicing and glad!"

## Joy Comes With The Morning
## Psalm 30:1-5, 11-12 (A Psalm Of New Orientation)

**Notes of the Psalms of New Orientation**

There is movement in the psalms of new orientation. They are not static like the psalms of orientation, but come alive with confidence that having been "through the valley of the shadow of death" we are now better off than before. These psalms presuppose a certain condition of life which no longer exists, which has now moved to something else.

In the case of the psalms of disorientation, the movement is from orderliness and goodness to disorder and suffering. Now in the psalms of new orientation, the movement is from how troubled life was to how God has restored his holy rule once again. Emotionally the speaker moves from being stuck in life to becoming "unstuck." Life can be lived once more because God has chosen to work the miracle of transformation among his people. These psalms celebrate the victory of good triumphing over evil.

**Hymn No. 1**

Psalm 96 (Tune: Lasst Unns Erfreuen, "From All That Dwell Below The Skies")

O Sing to God a joyful song,
Come all on earth and join the throng.
    Blest are you, Lord, our creator.
You bring salvation day by day,
Both in our work and in our play.
    Blest are you, Lord, our creator,
    Alleluia, Alleluia, Alleluia.

Lord, all the nations praise your power.
They stand assembled in this hour.
   Great are you, Lord, King of nations.
Truth, power, majesty, and fame,
Beauty, and glory form your name.
   Great are you, Lord, King of nations.
   Alleluia, Alleluia, Alleluia.

All you who gather here to pray
Lift up your hearts and with us say:
   "Blest are you, Lord, our Redeemer."
Here in this court with love comply,
Offer your life, on God rely.
   Bless the Lord, our great Redeemer.
   Alleluia, Alleluia, Alleluia.

Let all creation burst in song,
Sea, field, and forest, teeming throng —
   We exalt you, living Savior.
Come, Holy Lord, and judge the earth,
O come in judgment, bring new birth.
   We exalt you, living Savior.
   Alleluia, Alleluia, Alleluia. Amen.

**Hymn No. 2**
Psalm 150 (Tune: Darwall's 148th, "Rejoice, The Lord Is
         King")

To you, our Holy God, We bring our praises strong.
We call on all to laud and sing your joyful song.
   Sing praise to God,
   Who is the sovereign of all things, O praise the Lord!

You rule with might and strength Above the firmament.
We call on all in heaven and earth to give assent.
   Sing praise to God,
   Who is the sovereign of all things, O praise the Lord!

We sing of power and strength Transcending time and space.
With trumpet, flute, with reed and pipe, engulf this place

To offer praise
To God, the sovereign of all things, O praise the Lord!

Let every living thing Join in this song of praise.
All creatures join and sing, praise God through all your days.
Sing praise to God,
Who is the sovereign of all things, O praise the
Lord! Amen.

**Hymn No. 3**
Psalm 116 (Tune: Forest Green, "All Beautiful The March
Of Days")

We love you, Lord, for you have heard Our cries of deep
distress;
You hear the anguish of our pleas, For this your name we bless.
Your name is merciful and right, And love shines
from your face.
E'en in the lowest points of life You guard us with your grace.

From death, from tears, from stumbling feet, You keep our
lives secure;
While trust in others brings no help, With you we will not fear.
And so we set our feet to walk Your path within this land,
To follow you through any grief And trust your gracious hand.

Within this house we lift our hearts, Our lives we promise now.
This sacrifice of thanks and praise, Here Lord receive our vow.
As you have fed us in this place, Now lead us past these
doors.
That all may learn to seek your face And serve you evermore.

And so we set our feet to walk Your path within this land.
To follow you through any grief And trust your gracious hand.
To you, the maker of us all, To you, the Risen Son,
To you, the Spirit of new life, We lift our hearts in song. Amen.

**Call to Worship:**
    **Leader:** Praise the Lord!
    **People:** Sing a new song to the Lord, praise him in the
                 assembly of his faithful people!

| | |
|---|---|
| **Leader:** | Be glad, Israel, because of your Creator; rejoice, people of Zion, because of your king! |
| **People:** | Praise his name with dancing; play drums and harps in praise of him. |
| **Leader:** | Let God's people rejoice in their triumph and sing joyfully all night long. |
| **People:** | Let them shout aloud as they praise God. This is the victory of God's people. Praise the Lord! |

(Psalm 149:1-3, 5-6, 9)

## Call to Confession:
This is the covenant which I will make with the house of Israel, says the Lord: I will put my law within them, and I will write it upon their hearts; I will be their God and they shall be my people. I will forgive their evil deeds, and I will remember their sin no more (Jeremiah 31:33-34). In penitence and faith, let us confess our sins to almighty God.

## Prayer of Confession: (Unison)
Have mercy on us, O God, in your loving-kindness. We have not loved you with a pure heart, nor have we loved our neighbor as ourselves. We have not done justice, loved kindness, or walked humbly with you, our God. Create in us a clean heart, O Lord, and renew a right spirit within us. Restore to us the joy of your salvation and sustain us forever with your bountiful Spirit. Amen.

## Declaration of Pardon:
For we know that Christ has been raised from death and will never die again — death will no longer rule over him. And so, because he died, sin has no power over him. He now lives in fellowship with God. Surely you know that when we were baptized into union with Christ we were baptized into union with his death. By our baptism we were buried with him and shared his death, in order that, just as Christ was raised from death by the glorious power of the Father, so also we might live a new life (Romans 6:3-4, 9-10).

**Hymn of Response:** (Please sing after the organist plays the melody once)

> Now let the heavens be joyful, let earth her song begin.
> Let the round world keep triumph and all that is therein.
> Let all things seen and unseen their notes of gladness blend,
> For Christ the Lord hath risen, our Joy that hath no end.
> Amen.

*(Note: The tune for this response is Lancashire, "The Day Of Resurrection!")*